WHAT'S SO FUNNY
ABOUT COMPUTERS?

WHAT'S SO FUNNY ABOUT COMPUTERS?

cartoons by

S. Harris

foreword by
Christopher Morgan

Los Altos, California
William Kaufmann, Inc.

To my father, Sol Harris, who is
quite a computer himself.

Library of Congress Cataloging in Publication Data

Harris, Sidney.
　　What's so funny about computers?

　　　1. Computers—Caricatures and cartoons.　　2. American
wit and humor, Pictorial.　　I. Title.
NC1429.H33315A4 1982　　　741.5'973　　　82-21227
ISBN 0-86576-049-7

Many of the individual cartoons in this book have been
previously published and copyrighted by: ABA Press,
*American Demographics, American Scientist, Chicago
Magazine, Chicago Tribune, Datamation, Discover, Dynamic
Years, Johns Hopkins Magazine, Phi Delta Kappan, Manage-
ment Review, Medical Tribune, Playboy, Science 80, Wall
Street Journal,* and *Saturday Review.* The cartoons on pages
5, 17, 28, 40, 48, 58, 100, and 115 were created for *Discover.*
The cartoon on page 109 is reproduced by special permis-
sion of *Playboy* magazine, copyright © 1977 by *Playboy.*

10 9 8 7 6 5 4 3 2 1

First Edition

Printed in the United States of America

FOREWORD

Cartoonists return year after year to mine the riches of a handful of classic themes: the desert island; the mad scientist; the "end of the world"; and, more recently, and of particular interest here, the computer cartoon.

Since the fifties cartoonists have burlesqued the computer by making fun of its supposedly humanlike petulance or by exploiting its ability to induce paranoia. You know the kind of cartoon: an electronics laboratory is filled with dozens of white-smocked attendants servicing a giant computer. The computer, fed up with taking orders and performing on cue, emits a strip of paper tape telling the technicians to "Say Please." And so on.

Well, that's fine as far as it goes. But most cartoonists are still living in the dark ages, computerwise. Today's new microcomputers are small, portable, friendly, and nonimposing. They're just as funny as their giant ancestors, but in a different sort of way. A small computer doesn't overpower the individual the way a room-sized monster does. Which is not to say a small computer can't induce paranoia, too. It can; but the nuances are different.

I have some firsthand knowledge of the contemporary cartoon situation: I edit *BYTE* and *Popular Computing*, two magazines devoted to microcomputers, and I get a lot of unsolicited cartoons over the transom from hopeful cartoonists. Unfortunately, most of them aren't funny. Sometimes it's because the cartoonist fails to realize that most of the new computers being bought today are small microcomputers; their work is still dominated by the old, giant-computer mentality. Or perhaps it's just that cartoons obey Sturgeon's First Law. Theodore Sturgeon, the science-fiction writer, was once confronted by someone who claimed that "Ninety percent of science fiction is totally worthless." (That's not exactly how the remark was phrased. I'm paraphrasing in the interest of decorum.) Sturgeon quickly agreed, adding that "Ninety percent of *everything* is totally worthless."

Computers are a particularly hard nut to crack. Computers are not inherently funny objects. Unlike other classic cartoon situations, the computer situation requires a good deal of wit to make the joke work.

Sidney Harris has that special kind of wit. For years he's been poking fun at the foibles of scientists and technical people, sometimes gently, sometimes not so gently. Sidney gives new meaning to the word "paranoia." His data base computers gobble up information quicker than you can say "freedom of information." His big computers are redoubtable; his small computers are pleasantly irascible. And he manages to make "big computer" cartoons timely and funny, too.

In speaking about editorial cartoons, John Oakes once said, "A cartoon, if it's good, has to be unfair." That applies to cartoons and satire in general. There's a nicely treacherous edge to some of Sidney's work that would turn up the corners of Machiavelli's mouth. But I like Sidney's more gentle efforts, too. One of my favorites is from another cartoon collection of his entitled, *What's So Funny about Science?* There's no caption: Einstein is shown in deep thought in front of a blackboard where he has written and scratched out two equations: $E = Ma^2$ and $E = Mb^2$.

Cartoons don't come any better than that.

–Christopher Morgan

"It says it's sick of doing things like inventories and payrolls, and it wants to make some breakthroughs in astrophysics."

"But remember—just because I said you were wrong
doesn't mean I don't love you."

4

"It says, 'Three percent split infinitives, 8 percent passive verbs, 16 percent compound-complex sentences, average sentence length 26 words, paperback rights $3.2 million, movie sales $8.3 million, total take $11.5 million, less 15 percent agent's fees.' "

"By putting all our data into code, our competitors can't read it, our unauthorized personnel can't read it, and, I'm afraid, neither can we."

"I can remember when all we needed was someone who could carve and someone who could sew."

"According to this theory, it's strongly improbable that anything should ever happen anytime, anywhere."

"You mene I've bin spending this whol term with a defektiv reeding machin?"

"The computer can talk to terminals all over the country. Bentley thinks it's talking about him."

"Everybody needs candy. Everybody needs
stationery. Everybody needs microcomputers."

" . . . and what's more, my databank has more data
than your databank."

"It says our line printer is obsolete, our remote terminal is obsolete, and, I'm afraid, *we're* obsolete."

15

"This is truly one of the great poems in the language.
Computerese, that is."

"No wonder he never forgets. He has a bubble memory with a storage capacity of 360 megabytes."

"True, *we* don't give out personal information, but every once in a while the computer takes it upon itself to spill the beans."

"The beauty of this system is that there are a few
small errors programmed into it, which helps to avoid
total depersonalization."

"Have you noticed that as these things work faster
and faster, we finish our day's work earlier and
earlier?"

"How do you want it—the crystal mumbo-jumbo or
statistical probability?"

"We have to be forthright with the public. We have to have their confidence. We have to convince them we're working for the common good. *Then* we can invade their privacy."

"Extrapolation is one thing. Picking the pennant winners is something entirely different."

"Their parents aren't going to be very happy with one of their predictions. They discovered that when they're ready for college, tuition will be around $18,000 a year."

"So much for Newton. Now, as for Einstein . . ."

"This homework is a disgrace. I'd like a note from your computer."

"Remember that code we couldn't decipher for seven years? We deciphered it—but do we want to know everything there is to know about rainfall in eastern Peru?"

"This is not what we meant, Snider, when we asked
for a thorough study of the laws of gravity."

"You can put away your translating calculator now.
I'm speaking to you in English."

"Sometimes I just feel like processing some data,
but I have no data to process—other times I have the
data, but I have nothing to process it with."

"If this machine isn't out of whack, reading is going to be even harder than I expected."

"I think we'll get a *third* opinion. My computer and I disagree."

"Wallace is making great use of his computer. He can tell you what the Bolivian tin exports will be for the next . . . what is it, Wallace, 67? . . . for the next 67 years."

"As I see it, it's a toss-up between a Belgian data processing machine and an American electronic computer."

"I know you struck out the first 26 batters, Fernando,
but the computer says we have to take you out."

"It does data processing, word processing and list processing. Get me some data, some words and some lists."

"This used to take hours."

"According to our home computer, we should buy some furniture."

"Why don't you check with the local databank?"

"This is not going to look too good on your record:
complaining about invasion of privacy."

"Sure it's depressing. This thing has a memory of 3 trillion bits, and I can't recall what I had for lunch."

"It's your computer. I'll have to call in a systems analyst."

"Now all this stuff will finally begin to pay for itself—
here's the formula for transmuting lead into gold."

"Say—according to our home computer, we're out of beer!"

"Take two aspirin."

52

"Dataholic."

"We have some facts about you that you don't remember, some that you thought were really secret, and some that never even happened."

"If automation ever creeps into *this* place, I'm getting out."

"We programmed it to simulate living conditions in the year 2000, and it's become hysterical."

"It was bound to happen—they're beginning to think like binary computers."

"No wonder you can't hear anything. You're plugged into your calculator."

"Tomorrow's prices."

"I know we seem perfect for each other, David, but
let's check it with a computer just to make sure."

"Say, Brown—take 14 years and check this answer."

"How many times must I tell you not to punch, bend, or mutilate your fellow workers!"

"Sure you can become a systems analyst if you want to—but tell Daddy, what *is* a systems analyst?"

"Now don't panic. Not *everything* was erased. We still have loads of data on rainfall, upholstery and jaywalking."

"This problem had been my life's work. I planned to
devote my remaining years to it. It's just been solved
in four seconds."

"Not bad for a computer, but the chimpanzee's work had more feeling."

"Yes, it computed the answer in a billionth of a
second and printed it instantly, but until I find my
glasses . . ."

"The central processing unit is on strike. How does one negotiate with a central processing unit?"

" . . . while 86 million prefer grilled cheese, and 58.7 million of *them* like mustard on it."

"Hello—goodbye."

"How nice. I didn't even know they *had* computers in
nursery schools."

" . . . and in 1/10,000th of a second, it can compound
the programmer's error 87,500 times!"

"It's not working because it claims it can think and has decided not to."

"Madge, did we really need a home computer to
make scrambled eggs?"

"It says, 'Teach me readin' and writin' because I'm
sick of 'rithmetic.' "

"Now with this system you can do the equivalent of running a steel mill—keeping track of the quality of the ore, domestic and foreign orders, smelting processes . . ."

"The problem seems to be in the memory bank."

"It hasn't helped their reading, but they've become
very proficient with computer hardware."

"The databank is slightly mistaken. I'm not an
alcoholic. I never attempted to assassinate the
governor. I haven't been married seventeen times.
I don't owe $86,000 in gambling debts . . ."

"All these delays—a thousandth of a second here, a
millionth of a second there. We'll have to get the
darn thing fixed."

"Another advantage is the humming and whirring,
which is so much more pleasant than chalk
screeching on a blackboard."

"Now that we're completely automated, there's no one to yell at."

"What it comes down to is this thing is capable of
telling us a lot more than we really want to know."

"I've got a home computer in my den and a desktop
computer in my office. Here, I feel lost."

"I think what we need now is someone called a computer programmer."

"Oh dear—Daddy's been replaced by a computer."

"Let's see now—a degree in computer science . . .
working for two years . . . Ah, I see you do well with
electronic games, with a high score of 280,000 in
Galactic Invasion."

"Sorry I'm late, but the databank had me confused with another Arvin K. Wheatly, and I was questioned by the authorities about smuggling arms to Afghanistan."

"For openers, your credit is lousy."

"If it wants to dream, we could give it some vague,
unstructured problem to mull over during the night."

"It can print information at the rate of 5,600 words
per minute. Run a help wanted ad for someone who
can read 5,600 words per minute."

"Since we got the microcomputer, Graham spends
an hour every night balancing the checkbook."

"It seems that *their* databank has all the information that's in *our* databank, plus information that's *not* in our databank, plus information *about* our databank."

"First you forget logarithms. Then you forget how to do long division. Then the multiplication table begins to go . . ."

"I'm firmly convinced that behind every great man is
a great computer."

"We're sponsored by a local computer company."

NAUGHTY
NICE
NICE
NAUGHTY
NICE

RACHEL ANTELL
CARL FURILLO
MICHELLE MONTOYA
BUD POWELL
HENRY MARTIN

S.Harris

"It's known as the KT-26, but you can call it 'Mom,' since it knows more about you than your mother does."

"What disturbs me most is the growing impersonality of daily life."

"Invasion of privacy."

"This one writes some fine lyrics, and the other one
has composed some beautiful music, but they just
don't seem to hit it off as collaborators."

"We've finally paid up on this $300,000 baby, and now they come up with one that can do the same job for $79.95."

109

"When you come over, bring your computer. We'll sit around and swap data."

"If to err is *human*, how do you explain *this* mess?"

"What I especially like about this baby is this little drawer where I can keep my lunch."

"What I appreciate even more than its remarkable speed and accuracy are the words of understanding and compassion I get from it."

"It goes on to say, 'The fault is not with the hardware. It is with you—the software!' "

"I sit here and solve mathematical problems, program electronic music, analyze architectural possibilities . . . but somehow being a Renaissance man isn't what it used to be."

"No, he doesn't have two desk top computers because he's so efficient—he has them because he's so insecure."

"We now have the ability to predict many events with much certainty. Unfortunately, most of them are elections."

"In a way it's encouraging, knowing they're not perfect."

About the Artist

According to Sidney Harris, the most asked questions of cartoonists are: Where do you get your ideas? and What size paper do you use? Harris hopes someone will come up with a unified theory on the subject, so that there will be one single answer to both questions.

Until then, he hopes to keep turning out his drawings on various subjects by following his own theory, which is not to let too much firsthand knowledge get in his way. To prove that point, he draws virtually no cartoons that depict life in a suburban neighborhood, such as the one in which he lives. All that might change, he claims, if and when the Dewey decimal people decide once and for all if cartoons are fiction or non-fiction.

It should be noted that, far from being typecast in the science field, Harris won an award from *Playboy* for having drawn what they selected as their best black and white cartoon of 1981.

Harris's previous books are: *So Far, So Good,* Playboy Press, 1971; *Pardon Me, Miss,* Dell, 1973; *What's So Funny About Science?,* 1977; *Chicken Soup and other medical matters,* 1979; and *All Ends Up,* 1980, all by William Kaufmann, Inc.